ALIVE

Lois Howard

SUNACUMEN PRESS
PALM SPRINGS, CA

Copyright Lois Batchelor Howard 2019
All rights reserved.
No part of this book may be used or reproduced by any means,
without the written permission of the author.
Contact: poetlois1@outlook.com.

Published by Sunacumen Press, Palm Springs, CA 92264
https://sunacumenpress.com

"Nodding Off" published in The Desert Woman, 2012
"January Ocean" published by the La Jolla Branch of The National
League of American Pen Women for a 2012 calendar, "Riding
The Waves Of Creativity"
"The Re-Living" published in Women's Voices Of The 21st Century, a book
by the Greenwich, CT, Branch of the NLAPW, 2013
"It's How You Look At It" published in The Back Forty, Tate Publishing,
2015
"After All These Years" published in The Back Forty, 2015
"The Summer Party" featured NLAPW.com as national poem of the week
"My Great Grandmother" published in Pennine Ink, UK, 2012
"Celestial" and "Their Dance Card" published in On The Face Of Things,
Finishing Line Press
"Lucille Clifton" and "Galway Kinnell" in POET Magazine, 1996
"Rotation" in Laguna Poets Series

Printed in U.S.A.
ISBN: 978-0-9995612-8-7

Poems Herein

Loved family, friends,
readers, old and new,
I hope some of these
will interest nice you.

The cover photo can be
sunset and sunrise.
Not until your reading
are these poems
A L I V E

Sun-warm thanks, Lois

Contents

Poems Herein	Front
Alive	9
Evolution	10
Myth O Logical	11
The Observer	12
Wait…Do I Sense A Breeze?	13
Poesy	14
My Great Grandmother in Canada	15
The Real Journey	17
It's How You Look At It	18
January Ocean	20
A Passage	21
Rotation	23
Life's Like That	24
The Vast Space	26
Nodding Off	27
Each Poetry	28
On Words	29
A Trick Of The Eye	31
After All These Years	32
The Lullaby Of Healing	34
Two Authors Tryst	35
Similar Scripts	36
The Poets	37
Hushed	38
Main Street	39
A La Dorothy Parker	40
Shall Inherit	41
Who Goes First?	42
A Sad Reflection	44
Pro-American	45
Solo Flight	47
Papyrus	48
The Re-Living	49
In California Sun	50

The Summer Party	51
Celestial	52
Of A Transformation	53
Pastures	54
The Rain Dance Answered	55
Yesterwhen	56
The Too Sad Visits	57
Songs Not Kept Inside	58
The Spring Spree	59
The Planting	60
Ahead Of Me	61
Thanksgiving Day	63
The Y2K Passengers	64
You	65
At The Nursing Home	66
The Thermal Pane	67
The Eternal Question	68
Summer East	69
The Making	70
Galway Kinnell	71
Lucille Clifton	72
In Some Measure	73
Their Dance Card	74
A Music	76
Not Cacophony	77
The Dressing Table	78
As Pirate	80
Nature Graffiti Removed	81
The Gift Horse	82
Night Thoughts	83
Between Verses	84
Moving	85
Our Palettes	86
The Decades	87
Rather Like Bird Watching	88
Over	89
Alive	90
Just Starting	91

and when	92
Hinges	93
contemplation	94
Busy	95
The Backyard Cactus	96
Long Ago	97
Government	98
is	99
I am	100
BEEcause	101
In A Lifetime Of Mealtimes	102
Theorems	104
Labor Day	105
Sold Out!	106
Transitions	107
Reality	108
Of Seasons	109
About the Author	111

Alive

The world has been
for millions of years
and in this time
this
I
this you
came to be.
I marvel at
the universe
and rejoice
there is a
me
and thee
and thee
and thee

Evolution

In this one lifetime
many lifetimes I have known
yet I remember clearly when
my mind I did not own
and I remember youth was mine
and youth was teasing there
I found I had to leave her
waiting on the stair
to don my wedding gown

And, oh, the lives I've known since then
too numerous to tell
but when wearing every one
each seemed to suit quite well;
the wedding gown is empty
the children are all grown
and I cannot name the lifetime
of lifetimes fully flown
or say exactly when

my mind became my own

Myth O Logical

A unicorn
using its horn
to dig into buried words
uproots them
and tosses them upwards

from the forest floor
the words propel
to the bellies
of computers
robot-run

synthesized and
sound recorded
the words
now one flow
spill forth

music
to listening animals
and
to the spell-cast
unicorn

unable to stop
using its horn
to unceasingly unearth
the unbounded treasure of
Words

The Observer

He covered the clock
with thick, rich, sticky honey,
and it wasn't long before the
sweetness attracted many flies,
so many it was almost impossible
to see the hands of the clock.
Then he smiled and quietly said,
"Times flies."

ALIVE

Wait…Do I Sense A Breeze?

I thought it would be so different, God.
I thought I'd set the world on fire, but
my sky is barren of heat and flame
and I am passionless and tired.
I do not mean to be ungrateful.
I am thankful for years of depth and fluff, but
why is it that what I have—or, more,
who I am—is never quite enough?
It seems to me, in truth,
that I am disappointed in me.
There was so much more I wanted to do,
so much more I wanted to be…
and now the time is narrowing
and my energy is low
yet here I am, asking for more,
a second wind before I go…

Poesy

Oh, to write like Ogden Nash!
That would make non-dancers dance.
"May I waltz with you, Ogden dear?"
"I hardly think that's why you're here.
You're here because you think
I will tell you secrets of my trade,
but I won't. It might make you afraid
of not having a voice of your own,
borrowing someone else's tone.
My advice to you is not to be carryin'
the desire to become a fun Ogdenarian.
You don't want to dance;
you want to sit down with pen.
(Well, I suppose it would be fine to dance now and then.)
I'll tell you what: why don't we do both?
Pretty yourself, and I'll get my coat,
But I'll only go if you look very dashing
And we say no more of Ogdening or Nashing."
(It was hard to agree, but I happily did
as onto the dance floor we inkily slid.)

ALIVE

My Great Grandmother in Canada

We used to sit next to each other
on an old, brown daybed
that had no back, no arms. I
did not want to sit quite that close
but the springs had long given out and
you slid towards the heaviest or first sitter,
though heavy she wasn't. She
was very thin and frail, and I
was very young...I
used to sit and watch her work
and, of all things,
listen to her stomach growl. I
never heard anything like it. It
could compete with the bubbliest of brooks. Perhaps
embarrassed that I was so vocal about it,
she would laugh softly and say it came with age,
and I would have a game and count how many times
the growls would talk and answer one another. Her
body was never warm. It was like a cool, refreshing rain. I
liked to look at her: her soft, neat white hair,
her gentle, pretty face,
her quiet, steady composure,
her skin, wrinkled with kindness...
but, most of all, it is her hands I see when I think of
her. I would stare at her skin and
marvel that it kept her inside in. Her
hands looked as if someone had
pulled a pale silk cloth taut, and her veins appeared
as if to leap out and join her tattingwork. She would
crochet yards and yards of the loveliest lace, and I would
revel in the alacrity of her long. unthinking fingers. We
were together perhaps only once a year as I grew up,
but each time, as all the relatives would exclaim, "My,

LOIS HOWARD

how you've grown!" she would feel my face
in her warm, particular way
with her cool, knowing hands
and she'd say, looking so pleased that
somehow I felt pleased, too, "My,
you are growing up to be such a lovely young lady." And
never once, in all those years, did she openly complain or say
she was sorry she was blind.

ALIVE

The Real Journey

In each of us
there is a loneliness
an unspoken longing
to find the place
our spirits are seeking

LOIS HOWARD

It's How You Look at It

You have to have a sense of humor to be old.
I know; I look in the mirror and am told
(I might add, with unkind reflection,
when what I wanted was mere affection)
that I am also far from young.
"Listen, mirror, please...please bite your tongue.
You are as old as I am, you know."
"Yes," said the mirror, "I've been telling you so."
"Shush," I say, "I find you upsetting."
It simply says, "You should be getting
into daily realism classes."
Ignoring, I say, 'Where are my glasses?
I'm done with you, (I haughtily deign)
and I'm leaving you...when I find my cane."
"You'll be back," the mirror grinned on,
Even tho' of me you're not overly fond.
Take your broken hip and your arthritic shoulders,
toss back your head and try to be bolder.
Forget when you turn you see cataracts;
age, you know, is just how you act."
"Easy to say, you're not in my skin
which, you've noticed, is overly thin,
and heart medicine makes my arms blue and brown.
What, dear life, what's going on?
And I cannot wear belts," I tearfully say,
"some things have dropped and are quite in my way.
I look like a scarecrow," I start to gulp.
"Look at my hair; it's standing straight up.
Too, I don't hear well and that's a real pain."
"Nonsense, "said mirror, "you hear music and rain."
To my saying nothing the mirror replies,
"Just think of it this way; you haven't yet died!
Besides, you do laugh more than a lot

ALIVE

and you're able to stand on this very spot.
Did you actually think you'd never grow old?
You're quite lucky to be here, I'm often told."
I had enough. The day was waiting for me.
I took Windex and sprayed…with more than great glee.
I hate getting philosophy from an old piece of glass
when, clearly reflecting, I'm such a young lass.

January Ocean

The herd of horses gallops
in a frenzy toward the shore
foamy manes billowing on
turquoise backs arching and
curving forward in thunderous motion
spewing white spray capes
of phantom riders into the wind.
A giant steed slows, canters
and lurches to a stop
lapping at my feet.
Shoeless I touch
its cooling hooves
and back and forth
we walk together
along the shore

A Passage

Seeing the cupola and the gate
I had to enter, and there I was,
in heaven…and in my own backyard.
I couldn't help but think on
the wondrous thought
that we create our own heaven on earth.
I knew I was experiencing a
heaven in my ways.
I am blessed that love is in my life
to and from me.
I have food; shelter;
I can think; I can do.
I am more than grateful,
But why are some of us
more blessed than others?
It surely is not understandable
and it is not fair.
All media attests to that.
Guns and greed and cruelty
are murdering breath and dreams.
All of my blood
cries out in thanks
that I am where I am,
but I am no more special
than those who hunger or
fear for their lives.
And I did not create my
heaven on earth;
it was just there… here.
Is another word for life
'circumstance?'
and why would that lovely
painting of a door

LOIS HOWARD

prompt these thoughts?
I quietly thank the artist
and keep the door open…

Rotation

In dark blue coals of night
the diamond of the day
adorns another site
as embers dance their way
across the hearth of earth
that in turn rocks and rests
and touches aged girth
of eyelid easts and wests
with silence soft or sound
muffled in star-sewn capes
that, floating, cascade down
and all things closely drape
   Man is ever of this scheme
    tapping known with wakened dream

Lois Howard

Life's Like That

We're at this movie, see
an' the picture has everythin' in it
love, babies, kisses, war, folks gettin'' sick, gettin' well
people laughin', dancing, drinkin' eatin', workin'
divorcin', marryin', prayin', cussin', sleepin'
kids playin'
an' me an' my friend are sittin' there
holdin' hands an' eatin' popcorn
an' grinnin'. We like each other a lot
so we do a lot of grinnin'
we laugh at the movie
sometimes we cry
in one part
right in the middle of a sentence, mind you
she gets up to go to the restroom
'least, that's where I think she's goin'
she doesn't come back an' she doesn't come back
what I'm sayin' is, she didn't come back
an' I couldn't leave my seat
I tried. God, how I tried
I wanted to know if she was okay
I wanted her to come back so bad
but I couldn't leave the seat
it was like I was glued to it or somethin'
more like cement
an' the movie won't stop
it just keeps goin'
planes, boats, trains, cars
everybody goin' someplace
an' everybody dyin' or havin' kids
an' then havin' lots of pain or good times
an' always lookin' or after somethin'
I try so hard to get out of this seat

ALIVE

but I can't, an' I have the worst feelin'
someone's feedin' me
god, someone is feedin' me
this young man and woman in white
are talkin' an' standin' by me
I don't get it. In a movie?
Spoon by spoon…an' I can't tell them to
shove off. I know, 'cuz I've been tryin'
an' there's a tube in me
how…when did I get a goddamn tube in me?
the movie…why won't someone turn it off?
it never stops…it just keeps goin' an
Sally's never comin' back
the picture is gettin' blurrier
I'm glad of that
it was hurtin' my eyes
so much goin' on an' so loud, so loud
hard to think in all this noise
wait, feels like I'm leavin' my seat, an'
someone is squeezin' my hand
o, my god, o, my god…Sally!
Sally, where have you been?
so softly she looks at me
like she's not even been gone
an' not even whisperin' she nods to the screen
why, I'll be damned if she didn't come back
jist in time for us to see another baby bein' born
an' God knows what else

The Vast Space

Somewhere between dark and dawn
I hold the world in my arms
and cradled together at great height
we move through the stars
in many light years
I an integral
of this course, this path,
movement ever ours.
It is the touching that
seems to change
for very gradually
I and my armful of globe
begin to slip away
each from each
imperceptibly
as if in slow motion
a kindness
so that
I might adjust to less matter and,
forgetting I had half expected to drop,
find it strangely but not strangely
a lifting.
Neither of us fall.
Only the outer bursts as a seed
and weightlessly
I fly into a new old dazzling light
that warms and shines and
places each me
somewhere between dark and dawn
holding the world in our arms
where cradled together
we again move through the stars
imprinted on found fossils
shining in the new day sun

Nodding Off

I am older now than at birth,
which is a very good thing to be
and my body sometimes feels
it does not belong to me.
I lie awake at night
and turn and toss in bed,
my neck not feeling strong enough
to lift my weary head.

So, without moving a hair or a thread,
and feeling none the lesser
I simply take my head right off
and place it on the dresser.
As you can well imagine
sleep comes quickly then.
Of course there's that waking problem
of putting it on again.

Each Poetry

I could believe in God for That alone—
the mind she used to sculpt from letters' stone
meters of thoughts that cannot be surpassed
and from their concept to all ages last.

I could believe in God for That alone—
the way she pared her words to cleanest bone
bones dry, as for Ezekiel, given breath,
we new life inhaling upon each death.

Emily Dickinson, not then yet of fame,
now touches some as drought by driven rain.
I could believe in God for That alone—
but God knew I needed children of my own

On Words

"I hate poetry," my daughter said;
"Why can't you just say, 'It's raining?'
Why do you have to say
Zeus slid down shards of glistening silver
into the tormented moans of dark?
Why can't you say, 'It is raining?'"

"But you already know that, dear;
isn't it more interesting to see
a picture painted in colorful words?
Which would you rather be:
a Caucasian, female, twenty-nine
or

a ballerina poised on toe,
the white of your face
matching the white of your tulle,
glitter sewn to your cape to lift you
into a third decade on
fragile, stretching wings?"

"Mother, you know what I mean;
very few people talk the way poets write."
"True… and more's the sorrow;
shall we then, dear daughter,
save this issue
for a morrow?"

"See what I mean?" she said.
"It's close to irritating…upsetting;
your search for words is…is…is a fright;
and I have no solution for this madness;
Mother, dear,
Goodnight."

"Goodnight, Dearest Child;
sometimes...sometimes when you sleep
I feel the lining of my womb again exult
your name...I am so glad you came!"
"Oh, I must be in trouble, Mother; I'm beginning
 to understand...

and it's okay not to rhyme?"
"Anytime!" we say together, she adding,
"Hand me a pencil, Mom..."
THE END
or
THE BEGINNING...

A Trick of the Eye

Memories
sometimes surprise you.
Looking down from the plane at
the flat, quilted mid-west earth,
the land becomes
a floor full of wooden puzzles
and I can hear
my now grown children's laughter
and see them
placing parts in spaces
as quickly as this plane…
and years…
can fly

LOIS HOWARD

After All These Years

When you lose a child
there is nothing to grasp
You are in a vast void
you have nothing to hold onto
you look down and after a long time
you grab a wall that is
 unexpectedly there
but your hands keep sliding down
Faith doesn't always keep you up
You look down but you cannot see
 any end of the down
and it is freezing; you begin to shake
and you realize you are suddenly in water
salty; it is coming from your eyes and your pores
You try to climb the slippery wall
your breath comes and goes
and you realize you have to be making some headway
as the opening at the top has gone from dark to light
many times; you have forgotten how to count
You just know you have to keep holding the wall
Her loved voice is swimming in your ears
your hands and body now feeling
you are holding the wall up.
All you know is you cannot fall and you are going
crazy that your child died. You cannot accept that
she is really gone. Gone... Where is her breath?
You do learn to think in this deep well
You long for her live self. If only you can inch to
the top she may be waiting for you
You reach the day's full light and there she is
She grasps your hands, pulls you up and you embrace
There is a part of you that knows it isn't real, but
it is what you want to see and feel

ALIVE

Her voice fills the space. If I expected to hear her
say anything it would not have started with
"It's hard to describe the flowers, Mom."
"Oh, I love you, honey
we all do; we miss you so." That great big smile of hers
and then she was gone…gone, but not in spirit or heart
Soon after that I found myself planting flowers again
the birds of paradise blood orange in the hot desert sun.

LOIS HOWARD

The Lullaby of Healing

There is the lobbing,
lobbing of the water 'gainst the dock
there is the rocking,
rocking, rocking of the boat upon the waves
there is the thumping,
thumping, thumping of the footsteps
on the pier
and there is the beating,
beating, beating of my heart into the air

there is the wafting,
wafting, wafting of the fronds into the breeze
there is the edging,
edging, edging of the snail across the sand
there is the flooding,
flooding, flooding of the tide toward the shore
and there is sunning,
sunning, sunning shining through despair

Two Authors Tryst, In Amherst, England

"Love, I taste a liquor never brewed…"
"Aye, with devotion's visage…we do sugar o'er the devil himself."
"The earth was made for lovers…"
"Then come kiss me, sweet and twenty, youth's a stuff will not endure."
"Love can do all but raise the dead…"
"Give me your hand and let me feel…"
"O! Willie! O!…If music be the food of love, play on."
"Wait! Fair Emily, didst thou not tread upon mine line?"

LOIS HOWARD

Similar Scripts

On the sloping hillside
in the bright sunlight
the bird-shadow circles
practicing penmanship
on its parched land

Looking up from my parchment
I see the hawk
in its sweeping search
each of us writing
with comparable élan

ALIVE

The Poets

From my window above the sidewalk café
I can take in a part of the world
I knew first-hand years, years ago,
and looking at it from here...
from where we were and from where we are.
I watch them gather to share the seeds of knowledge
that kept us going, growing, gathering.
They usually arrive one by one, but
today is different from some.
Curiously, today they are dressed alike.
I cannot believe it; surely they must be gathering here
and then going on to a more formal affair.
They are in dark brown tuxedos—and it not noon yet!—
each wearing a tan vest and in such a number
an almost laughable appearance,
their berets crested black and pulled down
so flat upon their heads.
And they keep nodding to each other, like they
always did, eyes bright and knowing...
Are they discussing Baudelaire, Simone de Beauvoir,
Paul Sartre, Guy de Maupassant?
I wish I could hear them; I wish I knew what they are saying.
I miss being with them. how I miss being with them.
I, too, always found their company stimulating.
"No, don't leave yet; stay a while, stay," I beg through my
streaked, muted window, but as quickly as they arrived,
they are gone.
Gone. They have flown. Oh, how I hope the
Cedar Waxwings in their formal attire
now well may be singing for you

Hushed

There came that day
I found what I sought
silence
and of the silence was
a stillness in which
a magician
unseen by me
began to pull folds of scarves
from my storing heart
and in this silence
I could see not only the colors
but
the shimmering of the stars
the gazing of the moon
the brushstroking of the dawns
the golding of the sun
grass growing
flowers opening
leaves and prayers holding on
and through myriad eyes
lights! lights in that day
that day of centuries
lights shining the marvel of silence,
its song!
A song wordlessly wondrous
one that both gives and
takes your breath away
and once heard
it is yours to billow
on your own floating scarves
and
with the silence
Sing!

Main Street

It isn't the passing through.
We all pass through.
It is the slowing,
the stopping long enough
to share the
You of You.
It is the "behind the scenes"
that makes the passing through.

Persons gather in twos
or any number
and in the slumber
of fast pace
there are those moments
face to face
when each sees the
Me of Me.

We cannot always
just go through or 'round
in cities that are full of corner towns
to find and feel the pulse
that takes a slowing,
sometimes a stopping,
and in the times most plain
we know most gain.

"I would not have missed this
for the world," was said;
"This is the world."
And in such passings
each I
is fed
and flags unfurl.

A La Dorothy Parker

We were drinking warm coffee together;
He gazed at me sighing, "Let's hot it up!"
Excited, I started to remove my robe.
"Dear," he said, "I mean our coffee cups."

"Do you want to? Let's!" he said.
"Do I!" replied eager I.
He motioned to the waitress,
"Two orders of apple pie."
"I thought you meant something else,
that you later wanted passionate love."
"Darling, you know I have a headache.
Is sex-sex-sex all you think of?"
The apple pie was disappointingly good.

I wish he could always be around,
but his work he cannot quit.
Still, if he were always here
would I wish the opposite?

Shall Inherit

The way the winding road ran
the high California wildflowers growing alongside
I could only see the backs of the lambs
and I did not recall
lambs grazing there before

Looking back in the rearview mirror
to get a wanted second glance
several of the lambs
to my astonishment, stood,
and in their summer white shirts

the migrant workers bent again
low over the earth
with the sun
and breath of dreams
hot upon their backs

Who Goes First?

I could hear my boys
playing outside the window.
Well, not playing exactly…
"You started it," one yelled;
"You started it, you know you did."
The other hollered back
"Did not"
"Did"
And then it went quiet,
too quiet.
I went to the window
and looked out.
There were bodies everywhere
motionless bodies
everywhere….
Only the 'play clothes' were different.
"Get up, get up," I sobbed;
"It's time for you to come in for lunch."
The bodies did not move and
I pounded, pounded, pounded
on the pane.
The window clouded over with rain
and I stood frozen
wondering how my sons
went from playing war
to this war.
A TV voice stated how many dead
And I was able to say aloud
"How would our leaders feel if
their son or daughter were lying there?"
But that doesn't —or rarely—happens and
that wouldn't make it any better.
It wouldn't.

ALIVE

"We started it," I scream.
"Did not," the news reporter decisively says.
"Did," I scream back.
The downpour keeps falling from my eyes
that never again will see
my sons playing…

A Sad Reflection

We used to kind of make fun of Miss America
when we saw the competition on TV. My
brother would holler from the kitchen and mockingly
ask, "Has she said yet that she wants world peace?"
"Like they know anything about it," my sister would
shout back. "They all say that," the boy from next door
chimed in. We would laugh and loved each time it
happened. Dad would slap his knee and we'd almost
say in unison, "See?"

How we all enjoyed that evening,
drinking cokes, eating popcorn, rooting for our state,
and waiting for another contestant to say that what she
most wanted was world peace…and we couldn't wait to
see who would walk on the runway with a crown upon
her head, tears streaming down a happy face

Decades since
I wonder how we could have been so small-minded and
unknowing… for who would have thought then that one day
we would realize Miss America's words outdid our world
leaders…
war wears no crown…
draped flags bring our dead home…
there are no happy faces…
there are streaming tears…
tears crying for peace
crying for peace

ALIVE

Pro-American

It is morning and
the sky is touched with pink,
a streak of almost-red running through…

TV sets are blaring
and the news of the war
is unsettling, disturbing, heart-wrenching.
Pictures of protestors fill the screens
and a voice says
"The war is more than begun.
Our servicemen and women are deep
in the throes of war.
Don't protest now that the war is."

"You can still stop," the groups said.
"Stop before we encircle Baghdad and
ground-fight, ally to enemy…
Thousands more will die…
innocent victims, women, children, men…"

"You don't understand," the voice continues;
"You don't just stop a war.
We must save face.
We have to save face."

Too few faces have been saved.
The earth has become
a veritable garden of human faces,
faces looking in every direction,
bodies as reeds bending in the wind,
many eyes death-glazed.

LOIS HOWARD

It is evening and
the sky is touched with pink,
streaks of almost-red running through…
the stained earth
mirroring the sky,
the sounds of protestors and advocates
a cacophony not heard
here…

Solo Flight

Were I to write a poem today
what would I say?
That I am feeling low
and that the weeping willow bough
bows slightly in the arrow'd air
that I have made more humid being there?
And unaware of weight or me
or that the twig too weak might be
the yellow finch lands and holds most taut
as its unflying body seems to dance off
into its air ballet quite selfmade
not moving from its leafy stage,
the thin branch bending from its size
as I in my self-pitying guise
then see the bird fly and the branch lift,
mine the observed lesson gift:
There is a time to hold on and a time to go,
the same air offering more than we know.

Papyrus

In the depression
in the cold Buffalo winds
Mother stayed up nights sewing
to make me a suitcase of doll clothes;
she had wanted so much for me to like them
and she expected I would.
I was told I barely glanced at the suitcase.
Later I had paper dolls I do remember;
I liked books; perhaps that was the connection,
the feeling of paper, the cutting out,
the folding of tabs,
the choosing of paper cloth endless
in the drawing and coloring of your own designs…

Now decades later it seems so odd
so out of context and so not
to be remembering paper dolls
as I touch my frail mother's paper thin frame
bending the tabs of clean linen
across her paper skin shoulders
scotch taping her worn thin paper-fragile heart
praying that this favorite cutout
won't curl at the edges
or blow away in the cold Buffalo winds
my full suitcase again barely glanced at
leaning against her still bed
of dreams both found and wanting

ALIVE

The Re-Living

Through lips of frail face
for the countless number
she tells her story
as if for the first time.
I grow to wish she wouldn't
and then I find I am somehow
drawn into this drama.
It is like a play on Broadway
each performance, in repeating,
building a 'long run,"
the drama extended.
"Did I tell you when I was in school?
It was the one-room school and…"
"Yes," I say, knowing
she will continue, regardless,
"and the teacher
asked me to come early and
help her with the wood for the stove and…"
We have rehearsed. And rehearsed.
I listen and nod and stay,
"Yes, I remember," adding
"and you walked three miles to school."
"Oh, did I tell you that?" she asks. "Good!"
She goes on.
In the going on and going over
I am struck that
perhaps that is what keeps her here!
And we who are somewhat younger
will only later know
the touch of magic in it.

LOIS HOWARD

In California Sun

The February flowers break through
the snow of my winter mind
and I am touched by
fields and crevices of
possibilities
strength
joy
the color
each of us gives to life

With outstretched arms
I gather the flowers
with my eyes
and bring them
indoors
where
unseen
they fill my
every room

ALIVE

The Summer Party

I look into the corner
of my backyard
and the green and flowering
plants
are huddled together.
They look like a cocktail party
with too many guests.
Whom shall I uninvite?
Shears in my hand I approach
the foxtail lily desert candles
the wall germandus
the fairy bells
the bougainvillea
I know this is rude to say to them,
but I do. "It is too crowded here."
They laugh and I hear their thoughts
become audible in the late afternoon sun,
"but none of us wants to leave."
I look at my shears, put them down,
and return with a cocktail to join them.

Celestial

The stars looked down, fascinated.
They were overcome
with the beauty of the night.
"It seems as if one can see forever," the one said.
"Yes," sighed the other, nestling closer to him,
"it staggers the imagination;
there are far too many to count."
"Kind of like grains of sand," he said.
"Kind of, but golden, far more sparkly;
they just glitter, don't they?"
"Their constellations do give off unique auras,
much like the milky way."
"Do you think so?" she asked;
"I can't get over how lovely they are."
"Some look alike, but I hear they are like we are,
each one totally different."
"And they shine, many absolutely shine.
What are they called?" she asked.
"Human beings…people," he said;
some say they are bits of stars."
"Really?" she asked wistfully.
"Whatever, I just know
they make the night, the air, the vastness,
so very beautiful."
"Don't go in just yet," he said. "Let's stay out
and gaze at them a little longer."
They stood for what seemed moments or millenniums.
Then she was the first to break the stillness.
"Wondrous," she sighed.
"Credible," he said,
"Absolutely credible."

Of A Transformation

Looking out through
the long soaked window
the bare tree stood tall
against the grey, murky sky
and on each twig
beads of rain held on
rows and rows of beads
the trunk of the tree
now a large, brown vase
of iridescent pussy-willows
showering the assurance of
Spring

Pastures

When we were young
we touched the cows' charged fence
and almost in delight of pain
we jumped and shrieked and carried on.

Decades hence from then removed
the fence is far more real;
the stolid cows seem safe enough
and the current is not gone.

It runs throughout our lives
in jolts and bolts and flow
and for its intensities
could we but barter, pawn…

Now there's no delight in pain;
it boldly insists on lasting long…
but there are also songs quite sweet
and joys as strong

The cows learn very quickly;
others of us wait past dawns.
We keep jumping charged fences,
for life goes on.…

The Rain Dance Answered

The fairies are dancing again on the leaves
their raiment nothing but water
and undaunted by the falling rain
you can almost hear their laughter

Some hang on about to move
while others appear to leap
touched by light I cannot see
as tears not meant to weep

Theirs must be wondrous music
and in only major keys
as nothing in the minor
their dancing does appease

On twigs here branches there
hundreds of dancing lights
defy the greyness of the stage
bulbless they light day's night

in this free noontime show
as they plie and pas de deux
all attired the very same
in moist translucent hues

alone in my dry theatre
mesmerized by the fairies' gauze
they dance on, oblivious
that I break into applause

LOIS HOWARD

Yesterwhen

...words have not inked from my pen since
yesterwhen...
yesterwhen anything the huckster sold
was "sweet as sugar," fresh or old
yesterwhen hot coffee steeped with filling cream
yesterwhen all the days dreamed dreams of dreaming dreams
yesterwhen we, young, mirror gazed and preened and
yesterwhen became the now wherein we lean
on canes of breath
praying sweet death
take its sweet cyme
to yet sweetly smell
and friends to listen to and tell
our stories...ah, our stories of yesterwhen
we knew we'd never die
that all of life did sweetly lie
before us
and we learned 'twas worth the fuss
yesterwhen ink wells were high
with hopes and plans and eager sighs
and each day still is more of that
the faltering cane not altering fact
that sweet is life that bleeds from pen
in sweetest now or yesterwhen...

The Too Sad Visits

The buttercup is all that's left
I know; I've looked before
before the cobwebs for the years
unbroken cross the door,
before the gardener reckoned
and dug as if to bury.
I only come here sometimes
I find I cannot tarry

LOIS HOWARD

Songs Not Kept Inside

You hear it a lot,
but you don't always believe
that you feel the same
as young and old weave
the years into one,
your inner untouched
as, except for your skin,
you haven't aged much
inside the old self.
Your child lives there still,
surprised at the wrinkles,
not the body now filled
with memories rich
and some dreams found.
The body may slow, but
Inside-youth sounds!
You feel little different, for
your you is yet young.
And to have known both,
ah, our songs we have sung.
In this life game
of ever beginning
we know from experience
we are to keep singing.

The Spring Spree

The window at one end of my enclosed porch
is like a page in a book that I cannot put down.
Today's page was riveting, but too brief.
The doe and her fawn appeared on the hillside
as if stepping out of a movie reel.
The doe ran ahead and the fawn would scurry
to catch up,
thin legs frolicking beneath the bobbing tuft of tail,
and each time the fawn would reach the mother
the doe would again run even faster, it seemed,
the gap increasing between them,
though both were running faster,
the fawn always catching up before the doe
would go on
from one hiding cluster of green to the next
until they gamboled right off my page
into someone else's book.

LOIS HOWARD

The Planting

Morning glories, you get around!
You were seeded in just one space of ground
but, ah, that was not enough for you
you've invaded the lawn quite through and through
you flower in the peach tree and around the rose vines
and seemingly wherever the sunshine winds
you've circled the bougainvillea and have climbed the wall
you blossom on the hillside and the cedar tall
Why, your trail and logo of purple blue
colors almost everything that is in view.
Oh, morning glories, morning glories, morning glories
I once had a love like you

ALIVE

Ahead Of Me

"Someday," he said,
stroking my arms downward and
interlocking his fingers with mine,
"Someday," he softly went on,
"You will not remember my name."
"That can never, ever be,"
I whispered in return,
as deadly sure of this as
knowing my own face and
wanting his always near mine.
My whole body cried out to him.
He was the world.
Without him there could be no world.
The parts of me I could not see—
my pounding heart, my pulsing blood—
ached for him; I no longer was a body.
We were all the space there was,
I invisible to my self save for the passion,
this passion that swept me into knowing
we had found what no one ever knew before.
But…how long, how long ago was that?
This morning… surely not decades since…
lying alone in my bed,
I suddenly remember that moment…
his face, his touch,
the desire I thought would never leave—
for love just doesn't up and go
when it has caught you and
lifted your churning heart and stomach
higher than the stars butterflying
in the full, full air… It doesn't, does it?
But here I am, here I am.

LOIS HOWARD

It is dreams later, the world is still here,
and for the life of me, the very life me—
I've been racking my brain for hours now—
no matter how hard I try, I cannot,
I simply cannot remember his name...
and, it's funny...I wonder,
I wonder how he knew...

Thanksgiving Day

Listening to the silence
is a gift of God
for were I to hear the crocus
first debut through the sod

my feathers would be ruffled
as even sound so hushed
today would jar my swirling head
where thoughts have broken rushed

There comes a need in persons
to stop the outside sounds
so as to hear the way within
where given breath abounds

Today the gift to meld is mine
silence has chosen to visit
and perhaps it means even more
because silence—I mostly miss it

So in the brief caught stillness
which today has graced as mine
I thank God for such medicine
and at His banquet dine

LOIS HOWARD

The Y2K Passengers

We fly in the Now
the past
becoming smaller and smaller
disappearing in the midst,
the nose of the plane
parting the future
with resolve of steel and
sure, steady speed,
the Nows each already new
vainly
competing with
future
always ahead
oblivious of years
etched in calendars
or
mountains
worn by tens of centuries

You

You came as if always in my life
and loved me madly, gently.
You came as if always in my life, and
promised not to go away.
The sun did not always shine
and skies were not always blue
but through the flood of years
there was your promise.
There was You
 loving me madly, gently,
 loving me madly, gently,
 we, loving each other madly, gently,
 through the mad and gentle years…

LOIS HOWARD

At The Nursing Home

From the window, as it is,
and from the chair, as it is,
I can only see so high:
a bit of the mountain near its base and no sky

Nor can I see the birds…
but the shadow of the lone birds
in cursive flight across
this glassed California page
come and go
and leave no trace
upon the red parchment soil,
no brush dipped in lasting ink or oil

The window and chair only so big
and the flight if the birds so swift
a bit of sadness often flies in
uninvited
and somehow hovers
this side of the windowpane
a sadness that faceless shadows
can neither lift nor chain

One cannot have shadows without light…still…
so many lives here and gone without a trace…
How many shadows, I wonder,
have crossed this shadowed space?

ALIVE

The Thermal Pane

A glass door
at one end of the Nursing Home
faces the street over which I often drive and
today as I sat at the red light
I saw two very old people inside
each sitting in a wheelchair by the door
heads slightly tipped back, mouths open

One chair was faced
directly toward the door and
the many passing motorists,
the other chair sideways
facing an immediate wall

I wondered what type of person
would place a man
so that he could see nothing.
Then even from that distance
I thought the eyes were vacuous

Will there come a time
for some of us
when it does not matter
which direction we are facing?

LOIS HOWARD

The Eternal Question

Papers and years…
philosophers, historians, mystics
many a person
wondering, seeking,
papers ripped from tablets
some wrinkled, torn,
stained, yellow'd
thoughts climbing walls
and decades of minds…
What is this all about?
Papers and years…
A gentleman
quietly speaks up.
His words invite
acceptance:
He simply says,
"Life is what it is."

Summer East

Sitting at the table
in the warm climate
the waiter said,
"And for dessert we have pie."

"What kind?" we blithely asked
as the sun spilled on
the open porch.
"You've forgotten it's July?"

Looking at each other
we watched as he took
a hot and sticky knife;
"It's something you can't quite see.

It is a Chef Special
at this time of year."
And from the sky
he served us…humidity.

LOIS HOWARD

The Making

God, you don't have to go far to find poems.
They breathe from the nests
where they warm their eggs;
they fly from the trees and
taste the nectar,
drink from the fountains,
skim the pool,
find the worm to feed their hatched,
evade the cat
(just wanting to know
if you're paying attention)
and fly through the skies,
watching the hawk,
carefully watching the hawk
hover
circle
and
strike

more poems found

ALIVE

Galway Kinnell

Sun lit on the white bark branches
cottonwoods, perhaps
giving them a silver sheen

green leaves lifted in the gentle breeze
casting silver turns
to shadow-dance upon the windows' supporting beams

The poet's silver hair caught in light
and sun glinted on
his eye-glasses and his words

I catch my breath
I touch my silver
and suddenly I know the flight of evening birds

can be sun lit

Lucille Clifton

She is standing
where the others stood
before the same window
and the same tree
vital and majestic this day
full of waving branches
holding arms of ages
circles in its inner trunk
telling years
as do her words
encircling us in sage spirit
daring us to climb for Sun

when one is in such a moment
one never can forget
for as surely as I'm telling you
the tree bowed

ALIVE

In Some Measure

I am called a poet.
Remarkable. I've always wanted to be one
And I think almost everyone is
in their thoughts or in the sum
of their days and years
as their lives, unexpressed
on paper or sung,
meter themselves forward
in an art that is everyone's,
whether in silence or with dreams.
Living itself is poetry
composed, performed,
listened to, or breathed in

LOIS HOWARD

Their Dance Card

With brown spotted hands
she held the mirror steady
and stepped into the
smooth, firm skin of her youth.
The scent of the gardenia
rushed from her sea-green
strapless tulle gown
past her young lineless neck
and invited her to dance. Dance.
He looked as unsure and
bright-eyed as she felt.
His left hand in her right
his right hand gently on her back
their feet awkwardly moved
and they shared the feeling
but not expressed, "So this
is how it feels to be this close."
They slowly turned and dipped
their bodies into new dreams
at the close of every dance.
The band was playing "Stardust,"
and a crepe paper streamer had
become loose at the ceiling's edge.
They stood very still and very close
and as he looked directly into her
green eyes, she dove into his blue
and began to swim. "I...I...I think
you're swell," he said.
She knew no one else
had ever felt this way before.
"Is it too late for hot chocolate?" he asked.
"Hot chocolate? That would be nice,"
she shyly said, wanting for any excuse

ALIVE

to extend the night. "I don't think my parents
would mind if we have some at the house;
The Sugar Bowl is probably closed by now."
He touched her hair
and brought her head against his,
their cheeks touching. The room spun.
"Hot chocolate, honey?" he asked.
She put down the mirror
and joined him at the kitchen table
their feet touching
on their old faded flowered linoleum.

A Music

I have longed for the quiet of this time
soft muted sounds to fill these once loud rooms
a fresh hushed air to feed the waiting blooms
silence enough to hear the old clock chime

bold energy to blossom forth in rhyme
pianissimo to inspire new tunes…
so dare I now say I like a noisy loom?
can solitude be what I really held most prime?

and why did I not know this in the din?
family, friends, loves cannot be replaced
this found truth now marks my inner pace
and unwritten songs I still will sing

ensemble, forte, rests:
not too late blessed

Not Cacophony

Music is in everything about you,
your walk the brisk pace of Schubert's Militaire,
your face as serene as a Debussy sheer calm
spreading to shine from your glistening sun'd hair;
your mind is complex and heavy with Brahms
or else as playful as Sullivan… Satie..
and in your eyes—oh, those dancing bright eyes—
Mozart speaks to those who can and cannot see.
Your house is as orderly and glorious as Bach
and, when loving, Wagner's close sounds steal near.
Your laugh! Chopin is strongly chording the keyboard,
Beethoven waiting for great passion or tear;
in your deep thinking, Liszt visits often, and
Vivaldi is known to have not missed a season;
Your pulse dances from Strauss to Andrew Lloyd Webber.
In fact, all composers are yours, within reason.

The curious thing I found as I wrote
is that you don't sing or play e'en one note,
but sounds live beyond the known greats alone.
You enrich life with a music your own,
the ensemble of all, individual tones.

LOIS HOWARD

The Dressing Table

Over the tiled rooftops
the mountainous skyline
appears as a backdrop
painted carefully on the
world's largest canvas.
The profiled mountains
gape upward,
their large and small noses
not visibly breathing,
their sunken eyes as in trance
staring straight above.
Some mouths are closed
in seeming contemplation.
Some yawn.
Still others are open
in conversation
their full stomachs
protruding and pouching
beneath
necks and chests
sloping in the heating sun,
their lifted legs and feet
sometimes becoming the
head of the next.
In stillness
they waited their turn for
The Dresser
who is constantly at work
creating and delighting in
boas, or tutus, or shawls
or in emphasizing
the rust blue-grey or
the lilac-brown of

ALIVE

his actors' long, extended
curvaceous, scantily clad bodies.
Surely The Dresser doesn't mind my taking
just one powder puff cloud
and dusting myself
in mountainous dreams

LOIS HOWARD

As Pirate

Each time I fly
the jewels are there
waiting.
Would that I could
bend down and
scoop up the gems
from their treasure chest
but they are rooted where they are:
in cities, in towns,
on houses, highways,
church windows, street poles,
store fronts, tall and small buildings,
office complexes, malls, hospitals,
vacant lots, college campuses,
gas stations, passing trains,
lone houses in the country,
tabernacles, ships at sea,
traffic signals, other planes…
Yes, would that I could bend down
and scoop up these shining gems….
ruby red, pearl white,
emerald green, topaz gold….
but at this dizzying height
it is far easier to rob diamonds
up here on the high seas
as I grab a handful of celestial stars
to light my way into
this lofty, dazzling
jewelry of night

Nature Graffiti Removed

Assigned to whitewash the walls
they bounded, one upon the other
to clean the ragged boulders

some washed high, others low
and the cliffs stood tall
in their pails of Pacific water

never tiring of the
washing waves
splashing upon their shoulders

LOIS HOWARD

The Gift-Horse

I have known
sixty minute hours
almost always
and they have
most often
been rich and good
Then I met you
and hours are now but
moments long
the song and
sense of you
keeping from view
time's hands.
Could I
but stop our clocks
I would
for at this rate
life will too quickly usher by
and tho' my 'fate'
the more great
in having had you flower hours
the selfish in me sighs
to time and thee:
Lie down
Oh please
lie down and
wait with me

Night Thoughts

Nature itself
is visibly wondrous
but that which is unseen
is more wondrous still

Churning

Sometimes our thoughts
become
wanted butter

Insomnia

We're all good at something
for heaven's sake
but I wish I weren't so good
at staying wide awake.

LOIS HOWARD

Between Verses

I found a pile of words, and they said to me, "Rhyme!"
and they jumped in my lap quite one at a time.
Well, actually, they leapt to my pen
and they slid to the tip time and again,
so I took them all to the well by the ink,
and they patiently said, "We'll wait while you think."
And here and now at them I'm fast staring
suddenly realizing they're meant for my wearing!
So, I gather them up and shape them as clothes,
tho' I do seem to have a few caught in my toes
as I walk around, word-covered, head to the knees…
words that sometimes only the Emperor sees!
…and you!

Moving

The now cold house is quite filled with the sound of living sleep
the metronomes of steady clocks their quiet vigil keep
the purring of the napping cat is as alarm to air
the cobwebs caught at ceiling's wall remind they'd not be there
if fireplace hearth were warming still to daylight's dawning edge
and plans of each were stretching new above cold floors and beds
but knowing air heavy hangs in the silence of songs sung
in a waiting expectancy of babies' nursing tongues
milking the space with youth again in children's laughing games
parental or befriending love offsetting times of pain
and always the slow growing, the fast going of the years,
old calendars and photo albums vehicles to "here…"
There's shuffling out the doorway with farewell touch to all
and seeing in the bright eyes of those passing rushing in
the fire and needed passion that dares stoke dreams to begin
and in touching of the shoulders there is a door shared sigh
age knowing and youth learning that dreams…
they never die

Our Palettes

As I see it,
we start out
with an empty canvas
...blank...
It is up to us to paint the picture.
We start at the edges, the corners,
and we work toward the middle
from all directions.
We get to choose
the colors we like
and whatever the texture—
oils, water pastels, pen and ink—
when the canvas is complete
it is our picture.

It doesn't matter if
the painting next to ours
is more brilliant or less dull;
that is their picture.
This is mine.
Mine.
You may be in it, but it is
mine.
The no longer empty canvas is
filling...
and I hold the brush

well, when it is not being guided
by the Oldest Hand

The Decades

Only dearer did the evening sky grow
only clearer did my evening heart glow
the colors muted to lavender, soft peach
and dreams yawning, moving within reach.
So like the evening sky am I
holding fast to sun's soft sigh

LOIS HOWARD

Rather Like Bird Watching

I saw the deer go into the thicket
and for such a long time
I have been waiting for it to emerge.
It does not reappear.
I wonder if it is asleep
or is it meeting its friend or mate
or is it nursing a fawn
or is it no longer breathing
or is it just resting and
perhaps dreaming deer dreams,
mentally grazing, unpreyed
on the open hillside of green?
I am sure the deer's name is
Poem
and I wait.

Over

I dropped a drop of words
upon the parchment
and the paper, a blotter,
absorbed the words.
I wanted to retrieve the words,
but they were gone.
I have to begin again
but I cannot, for I
cannot recapture my thoughts.
Now only the blotter knows.
Kinda' sounds like only
the shadow knows, huh?
Naturally, I hope that 'Over'
is spelled M-O-R-E!

Alive

This world has been
for millions of years
and in this time
this you
this me
came to be
I marvel at the universe
and rejoice there is
a me
and thee
and thee
and thee

Just Starting

How many parents have heard this
as they are driving out their driveways
and not yet into the road,
"Are we there yet?"
Out of the mouths of babes…

Perhaps young words
for an older query…
Where ARE we going
and will we know when we are
there?

and when

old sheet of paper
these words, my scribbling
'heard on stairwell'
where was I

'you pray for me
i pray for you
i want you pray for me
up on the mountain top
you won't come down
i want you pray for me
i want you pray for me'

many years pass
where was i
i wish I could
remember

ALIVE

Hinges

In the movie the captured woman
tried to escape by slowly removing the hinges
on the door and gradually that worked

another woman was grateful the hinges
on her door helped keep the door securely shut
and she could stay safely within

a friend of mine felt confident
the hinges on her locked jewelry chest
would help keep the lid tightly closed

grandfather threw open his tool box
slamming the hinges back and forth
going in and out of it during the day

the hinges on the car doors stay hidden
when closed, much like our skin covered
hinge-joints on elbows and knees

most hinges have pins
to make them operative
and that is where love comes in

two people are fondly hinged
pinned with a "limited angle of rotation
between them" when love lasts

there is much brass around love
doors and boxes opening and closing
holding fast to that which is solid

LOIS HOWARD

contemplation

we have been a couple
for almost three decades
our love works

he just said to me
we need reflection
that rather startled me

he asked me to come with him
and he led the way
to a nearby lake

where it was quiet
and we could talk together
he seemed serious

i kept wondering what he
wanted to reflect about
was something wrong between us

we stood by the lake's rim
the day rich in sun
look at that reflection he sighed

i was more than relieved
oh, this kind of reflection
and together we basked in doubles

the picture reproduced on the water
as beautiful as its onshore givers
tall trees, blossoms, clouds coloring the blue

we stayed until the sunlight camera turned off
then my love and I mirrored our awe as we
reflected on the beauty of reflections

Busy

I wonder
if my children
would notice if
I stopped emailing them

I haven't stopped noticing that
their texts, emails, calls, and visits
are fewer, and I wish
it were something not to notice

Ages and years
don't always blend
many of us
noticing

LOIS HOWARD

The Backyard Cactus

Yesterday's
penis-like stalk and bud
overnight
birth'd
and blossomed
a beautiful flower

Long Ago

Sometimes
our minds surprise us.
I thought of Gonny today,
Gonny who told me
if you don't get up early
you miss the best part
of the day. She would tell
me this while her pie was
in the oven and the floor
was scrubbed and drying
and she had this time
to write us.
Across a country
and lives since then
this morn we had a
beautiful cactus flower
blossom in the back yard
and nod to us through the window.
My love quickly took a picture of it.
An hour later we went back
to look at it again, and it
had folded back into itself too soon.
I wonder if Gonny would
be surprised to know
that a beautiful desert flower
reminded me of a most special
beautiful mother-in-law
and grandmother, Gonny the
mother of another long love…

Government

Politics
Corruption
Are they the same?
Is honesty really
non-existent?
Who is to be believed?
Should we be wary of everyone,
including ourselves,
for in thinking no one is honest
are we lying to ourselves
that there is not such a thing
as an honest politician?
Surely
there have to be some,
don't you think,
don't you think???
The scouts are out
and history is unfolding...
How many is 'some?'
Mark Twain may have
had it right?
Twain has many political quotes.
"An honest politician
is an oxymoron."
But a bit more optimistic,
"I suppose, just as an honest man
in politics shines more
than he would do elsewhere."
May our government somehow shine!

ALIVE

is

Nothing
is
forever

except
forever

LOIS HOWARD

I am

How many minutes does it take
to text or email a short message,
such as, "Thanks, got it."

We all have levels of being busy.
Can not a grown child send these words
to a parent? God, did their mothers

teach them nothing, no manners at all?
How I would hate to be that mother
but…

BEEcause

If I were a BEE
I would buzz
'cuzzz
I like all the colors
of the flowers.
They brighten the hours.
I love the YELLOW-
lemon jello…
I love the RED-
shiny sleds…
I love the ORANGE-
early morn…
I love the GREEN-
capes for queens…
I love the BLUE-
birds that flew…
I love the PURPLE-
pigeons' circles…
I love the BLACK-
sidewalk cracks…
I love the WHITES-
angels' kites…
I love the way ALL colors grow,
some making a BEE-oo-tiful bow.
So, to every flower, I buzz, buzz, buzz.
I drink in their colors as any BEE does…
but just because I am not a BEE
I still can see what a BEE can see.
And be where a BEE can be.
Shall we buzz together?!
Come BEE with me!

LOIS HOWARD

In A Lifetime Of Mealtimes

I have tasted
highs and lows
love, family
births, deaths
faith, doubt
friendships, hardships
calms, winds
fullness, hunger
work, laziness
play, idleness
acclaim, disregard
brightness, clouds
sounds, silence
success, failures
standing, falling
laughter, seriousness
thinking, emptiness
comfort, pain
busyness, stillness
hilarity, depression
creativity, dullness
stars, darkness
security, fear
strength, weakness
walking, stumbling
energy, enervation
knowing, ignorance
pride, envy
health, sickness
joy, sadness
wakefulness, sleep
stopping, continuing

ALIVE

sometimes the taste was bitter
more times it was flavorful and
tasted like 'more'
but either taste did not wait
for me or us to sit at the table
the food was served and
we had to eat to
live

LOIS HOWARD

Theorems

Shoulders
draped with decades
I wonder
were I to go back
would I
could I
now
understand
geometry?

Labor Day

1894 we doff
workers are being honored
a well-deserved day off

125 years later
now 2019
we play away on Labor Day
gratitude still seen

celebrated by many
in the United States
a throng beyond count
know why this day so rates

we relish that this day
has its annual due
many however feeling
more days we could make do!

LOIS HOWARD

Sold out!

The doors have become
openings in a long cylindrical bird feeder.
Those gathered for the show
have changed crowded lines
on sidewalks and around blocks
to waiting actively on
slender branches and twigs.
The doors are open
and those attending are rushing in.
The performance is a musical;
many of their friends are in it.
There is singing, dancing, and even
the stage is swaying back and forth.
The applause is air borne,
filling the theatre
with clapping wings.
"Seeds" is a huge hit,
promising to be a loved long-run.
We excitedly have season tickets!

Transition

You are now There,
Not Here.
Thank God that memories,
Like loved music,
Live on and
There is no end to
Either…

Reality

Nothing is important
everything is important
the littlest things
the biggest things
playing, working
holding hands
a first kiss
marriage, children
wishes, dreaming
staring into empty space
staring into fullness
realizing
our nothings can be
everything

Of Seasons

Each cycle has its Spring
an engagement ring
the courtship of winter
glistening diamonds
inviting summer breath
to 'Joseph coat' beneath
the snow white sky
heralding the verdure of Spring
the marriage complete
anniversary after anniversary
following and celebrating
nature
life

About the Author

Lois Batchelor Howard's poems have been published in various publications: Unity, The National League of American Pen Women's Pen Woman Magazine, The Desert Woman, Pennine Ink, UK, The Avocet, Grandmother Earth, The Plowman Anthology, Romantics Quarterly, and The Santa Fe New Mexican; Celebrating Poets Over Seventy, Tower Poetry Society, MacMaster University, Canada; Button Magazine, Oasis Journal, New Mexico Digest, and many other publications. Lois has been the grateful recipient of many writing awards. Most recently she published a novel, Captured Passions, through iUniverse, (2019) and has seen two of her Yorkshire Publishing Writing Prompts featured online, "The Whistler" and "Spring."

Lois has long been enriched by a lifetime interacting with musicians, writers, artists, family, friends, and students. She finds all people and all ages interesting, many evoking a poem or story. She plays the carillon, piano, and pipe organ, and has composed musicals for schools and churches and songs for various soloists. Accompanying singers, instrumentalists, directing choirs, and writing have been highlights in her life.

Lois has four lovely daughters, two great sons-in-law, and five equally wonderful grandchildren. She lives in Desert Hot Springs, CA, with Frank, her love of nineteen years.

LOIS HOWARD

www.ingramcontent.com/pod-product-compliance
Lightning Source LLC
Chambersburg PA
CBHW020428010526
44118CB00010B/474